NEW TESTAMENT INTRODUCTION

Stephen Motyer

Contents

C.B.   P.C.

CATHOLIC BOOK PUBLISHING CORP.
New Jersey

Jesus—The Reason for It All

The New Testament exists only because of Jesus of Nazareth. Though He wrote nothing Himself, He caused the New Testament—a collection of writings of such extraordinary quality that they have shaped world history, and continue to affect deeply the lives of those who read them.

Yet, strangely, less than half of the New Testament (47%) is directly concerned with the life and teaching of Jesus. The rest is taken up with descriptions of His effect on people after His death. Although the Gospels record His powerful impact on some individuals, His life actually ended in apparent failure.

But, after His death, that all changed. Suddenly there were thousands of disciples, and within a few years even the opponents of this new Jesus movement recognized that it caused "trouble all over the world" (Acts 17:6).

The Resurrection

Why this sudden change? The New Testament hinges around it, focusing the reason for it on Jesus' Resurrection from death. This is central to the literary phenomenon we call "the New Testament." For suddenly Jesus became the content of the message, rather than the source of it. Unlike other disciples of great teachers, the first Christian disciples, who wrote the New Testament, did not think of themselves as passers-on of tradition—the stories of His life and records of His teaching. Instead, they were proclaimers of the Savior, Who by His death and Resurrection had opened heaven to all.

It was not that the memories of Jesus' life were unimportant: the very presence of the Gospels in the New Testament shows how vital

A typical artist's impression of Jesus of Nazareth. But who was Jesus? What was He really like?

they were for the first Christians. But the remaining 53% of the New Testament, beginning with Acts, arises primarily from this conviction about His Resurrection and its significance. The early confessions of faith in (for instance) Philippians 2:6-11 or 1 Timothy 3:16 summarize the message beautifully.

So who was Jesus?

By its very structure, the New Testament compels its readers to decide whether they accept the Apostolic confession of Jesus as Savior and Lord. But that decision is not the only challenge issued by the New Testament. Those who make the confession are still faced with the challenge of history: who was Jesus?

In 1892 Martin Kähler, Professor of Theology at Leipzig, published a highly influential lecture entitled "The so-called historical Jesus and the real, biblical Christ." Worried by nineteenth-century attempts to write a psychological biography of Jesus, and thus to make Him "ordinary" and perhaps more acceptable, Kähler argued that we must see that the "real" Jesus (German: *geschichtlich*) not a reconstructed figure understood through the channels of historical research. He is simply the Jesus attested by the New Testament—the Savior and Lord.

Kähler's distinction is certainly attractive to Christians faced with awkward questions such as "How can we be sure that Jesus really was as the New Testament portrays Him?" It would be nice to reply, "That question doesn't concern me—because my faith rests not on what Jesus *was* but on what He is, the 'biblical Christ.' "

An unavoidable question

The difficulty is that the central New Testament confession is in the past tense: it is a confession that "Christ died for our sins, in accordance with the Scriptures, that He was buried and that He was raised to life on the third day . . ." (1 Corinthians 15:3-4). It explains the historical event of His death ("for our sins"). It claims that the hype about His Resurrection is not illusory but points to another real historical event of staggering significance. It then builds present-tense confession ("Jesus is Lord," 1 Corinthians 12:3) and future-tense confession ("The Day of the Lord will come," 1 Thessalonians 5:2) on this historical basis.

So Christians cannot avoid the challenge of the historical ques-

rabbi from Bible times. Jesus was not a typical rabbi.

A tomb with a roll-away stone. The New Testament hinges on Jesus' Resurrection.

on, "Did it really happen? Was Jesus really like that?," even though their faith may actually rest upon a living experience of the Holy Spirit in the present.

Current scholarship emphasizes three things about Jesus:

1. Jesus' Jewishness

In many ways we cannot understand Jesus without understanding the Jewish world in which He lived and ministered. And this is not just a matter of His cultural environment (the customs, religion, and politics of His day), but also of His theological thought-world. He clearly lived out of the Old Testament (as we call it), quoting and applying it as rabbis always did.

2. Jesus' newness

At the same time Jesus was not a typical rabbi, nor indeed a typical Jew. He did not engage in normal debate with other rabbis, but taught on His own authority, and claimed that the Scriptures had been fulfilled through Him uniquely (e.g., Matthew 5:17; Luke 4:21). People saw Him as some kind of new leader—but what exactly? It is fascinating that His contemporaries asked the same questions about Him as people do

today: Is He some kind of prophet? What kind, exactly? Is He a political deliverer? Or just a healer, using divine, or demonic, powers? Or is He no more than a sage, a wise man, with some good ideas—or perhaps with bad, deceptive ideas? What does He mean by calling Himself "the Son of Man" —or is He talking about someone

Comparative lengths of New Testament books

| Matthew |
| Mark |
| Luke |
| John |
| Acts |
| Romans |
| 1 & 2 Corinthians |
| Galatians |
| Ephesians |
| Philippians |
| Colossians |
| 1 & 2 Thessalonians |
| 1 & 2 Timothy |
| Titus |
| Philemon |
| Hebrews |
| James |
| 1 & 2 Peter |
| 1, 2 & 3 John |
| Jude |
| Revelation |

else? Can He be "the Christ"? Jesus was so puzzlingly unusual that it is perfectly understandable that when He predicted His own death and Resurrection, as the Gospels suggest, His disciples simply failed to grasp what He meant (e.g., Mark 9:9-10).

3. Jesus' Messianic awareness

This debate about the newness of Jesus shades over into what Jesus believed about Himself. Scholars are now in broad agreement that, in some sense, He must have thought of Himself as a Messiah-figure. But in what sense? Here agreement ends. He seems to have been willing to accept the title "Christ" (Mark 8:29-30), but what did He understand by this term? Modern questions and puzzles are paralleled by the variety of different interpretations of Him in the New Testament—amounting to a fascinating, kaleidoscopic presentation of one of the most powerful and intriguing people of all time.

He was made visible
in the flesh,
vindicated by the
Spirit, seen by angels,
proclaimed to the
Gentiles, believed in
throughout the world;
taken up in glory.
1 Timothy 3:16

Jesus' Life

Jesus was born in Bethlehem, in Judea, probably in 6 B.C. He lived most of His life in Galilee, became an itinerant preacher and healer in His mid-thirties, but was quickly executed for political sedition at the age of about thirty-eight. He left no writings and a small group of about 120 followers.

Hardly the stuff of religious revolution. How did this beginning produce such a world-changing result? We need to seek the real, inner quality of this life, by interrogating all the New Testament witnesses. We start by reflecting upon the basic facts.

Three crowded years

Jesus lived in obscurity in Nazareth, a tiny village in Galilee, until He began His public ministry, probably in A.D. 30. The story really begins in the previous year, as dated by Luke (Luke 3:1-2), when Jesus' cousin John "the Baptist" started a brief career as a prophet. Huge crowds flocked to hear him (Matthew 3:5), among them Jesus, Whose Baptism by John in the Jordan River marks the beginning of His ministry in all four Gospels.

The most likely broad chronology of Jesus' ministry is provided by John's Gospel, in which three Passovers are mentioned (including the Passover at which He was executed). The date of His death can fairly securely be fixed in April A.D. 31: so from some time in A.D. 29 until then, He traveled around Galilee, Samaria, and Judea (then under Roman rule). Occasionally he ventured outside traditional Jewish territory (Matthew 15:21; 16:13), but basically He confined Himself to "the lost sheep of Israel," as He put it (Matthew 10:6). He had remarkable powers of healing, which created a huge response. But all the Gospels agree that it was His teaching that captivated people, conveying a powerful sense of the mysterious significance of His own person.

Jesus' message

According to Matthew, Jesus' proclamation was the same as John the Baptist's: "Repent, for the Kingdom

A quiet stretch of the River Jordan, near the Sea of Galilee.

of heaven is close at hand" (Matthew 3:2; 4:17). But in fact Jesus put a different spin on this message, compared with John. "The Kingdom of God" (or "of heaven") was a potent idea for Jews, expressing their sense that their real King was God, and fueling their expectation that one day God Himself would come to deliver them from alien rule and establish them again as His Chosen People. So "the Kingdom of God is close at hand" was a message loaded with political freight—and revolutionary fervor.

Both John and Jesus tried to dampen political excitement. John emphasized the personal response of repentance, and he kept away from Jerusalem, where all messianic revolutionaries would press their cause. In addition, he pointed people away from himself to "One Who is coming after me" (Matthew 3:11), with Whom the Kingdom would really arrive. Similarly, Jesus refused openly to proclaim Himself as the Messiah, and avoided political arguments. Asked whether He supported Roman taxation (the hottest issue of all), He rerouted the question around duty to God (Luke

Cave beneath the modern Chapel of the Annunciation, Nazareth.

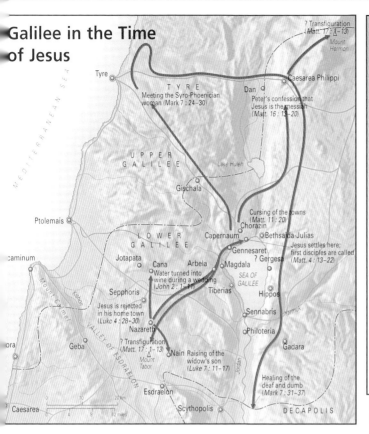

Galilee in the Time of Jesus

? Transfiguration
(Matt. 17 : 1–13)
Mount Hermon

Tyre

Caesarea Philippi

T Y R E
Meeting the Syro-Phoenician
woman (Mark 7 : 24–30)

Dan

Peter's confession that
Jesus is the messiah
(Matt. 16 : 13–20)

U P P E R
G A L I L E E

Lake Huleh

Gischala

Cursing of the towns
(Matt. 11 : 20)
Chorazin

Ptolemais

L O W E R
G A L I L E E

Capernaum

Bethsaida-Julias

Jesus settles here;
first disciples are called
(Matt. 4 : 13–22)

Gennesaret
? Gergesa

caminum

Jotapata

Cana   Arbela   Magdala

SEA OF
GALILEE

Water turned into
wine during a wedding
(John 2 : 1–11)

Sepphoris

Tiberias

Hippos

Jesus is rejected
in his home town
(Luke 4 : 28–30)

Sennabris

Nazareth

Philoteria

ora

Geba

? Transfiguration
(Matt. 17 : 1–13)

Mount
Tabor

Nain Raising of the
widow's son
(Luke 7 : 11–17)

Gadara

Healing of the
deaf and dumb
(Mark 7 : 31–37)

Esdraelon

Caesarea

Scythopolis

D E C A P O L I S

Star of Bethlehem

The best candidate for the famous "star of Bethlehem" is a syzygy, the configuration of the planets Mars, Jupiter, and Saturn in the constellation Pisces that occurred in the year 7 B.C.

:21-26). He broke religious taboos in reaching out to the outcast and "untouchables," and proclaimed a Kingdom in which the poor are blessed and the self-righteous condemned.

More than a prophet

But there came a moment when an excited Passover crowd wanted to make Jesus king (John 6:15). Jesus refused to precipitate an uprising. He preached a Kingdom of God that in one sense had come already (see e.g., Luke 17:20-21). And this is where we must consider that mysterious quality, that "extra" that set Jesus apart from John and all other prophets—a quality that people found very hard to define, but which led the first Christians to feel that in Jesus they had met God in a unique way. Whereas John told his disciples to fast in order to prepare for the Kingdom, Jesus and

His disciples feasted in celebration of its arrival (Mark 2:18-20). The sick were healed in fulfillment of the Scriptures, which promised the presence of God with His people (Matthew 11:2-6; Isaiah 35:4-6). Jesus forgave sins with divine authority—and people felt forgiven (Mark 2:1-12; Luke 7:36-50). He taught "as One Who had authority, and not as their scribes" (Matthew 7:29).

What gave Jesus these qualities? Was it simply the power of a unique personality? Or—the view that began to appeal to the religious authorities—was He able to exert demonic control over people (Luke 11:15; John 8:48)? In addition, the authorities began to feel threatened, as Jesus started to criticize them directly in the last year of His ministry (see Matthew 23; John 8:42-47).

Death and Resurrection

In this increasingly tense situation, Jesus began to predict His own death—but the Gospels are united in recording that He also predicted His Resurrection, and that He spoke of His death as "for the life of the world," "a ransom for many" (John 6:51; Mark 10:45; Luke 18:31-34). Is this just later Christian thinking read back on to His lips? In the search for the origin of the Christian view that Jesus' death was planned by God as a means of salvation, the best candidate is still that Jesus Himself began to speak of His death in this way—and expected His own Resurrection, in fulfillment of the same Scriptures that had already been fulfilled in part through His ministry.

He demanded, and received, a tremendous response from His disciples (Mark 10:28-31). And when the conviction of His Resurrection grew, this response became the heart—as we shall see—of all authentic Christian worship and living.

The Gospels

The four Gospels are the center-piece of the New Testament—indeed, of the Christian faith. Without them Christianity could not have developed as it did, for as a religion it depends absolutely on the historical claim that Jesus of Nazareth lived, taught, acted, died, and rose from death at a particular time and place, and that these events show Him to be Son of God and Savior.

So Christianity exposes itself to the fundamental challenge:

• *Are the Gospels reliable?* They clearly purport to be historical accounts of the life of Jesus, but does the claim stand critical scrutiny? This question quickly involves another:

• *What exactly are the Gospels?* We need to judge them on their own terms, and not ask them to conform to our requirements. And this in turn makes us ask:

• *Why are there four Gospels—and how should we understand the relationship among them?* At first sight, both the overlaps and differences between them set a question mark against their reliability.

What are the Gospels?

We start with the second question. In recent years a scholarly consensus (led by Dr. Richard Burridge, of King's College, London) has grown that the Gospels are examples of a genre, or type of writing, known as the "*Bios*" (Greek for "life"). The Greco-Roman "*Bios*" was typically a work of short to medium length (fitting on one papyrus roll), concentrating on an individual of special significance, whose story would be told through typical incidents revealing his or her character, drawing moral lessons to be learned, and focusing on the birth and death of the person concerned.

This immediately suggests that we should not ask the Gospels to provide a comprehensive biography of Jesus, minutely documenting the details of His life. Not "biography," but "*Bios*"—a broad-brush presentation—of the person through typical incidents that enable us to understand Him.

Why four Gospels?

A widely-given answer is that each Gospel was associated with an important Christian center, or with one of the leading Apostles. Hence, initially (this view suggests), each Gospel was written only for a limited circle—a single church or maybe a group of churches—to address their particular needs.

Recently this theory has be[en] attacked by a group of scholars l[ed] by Prof. Richard Bauckham of S[t.] Andrew's University. He points o[ut] that there was extensive conta[ct] between the earliest Christia[n] groups, and that it is high[ly] unlikely that the Gospel-writers, [as] authors of a "*Bios*," were trying [to] meet needs just in their ow[n] churches. And ancient book pr[o]duction was very haphazar[d.] Authors could not prescribe wh[o] might receive a copy or mak[e] further copies for friends.

Filling in the gaps

If Bauckham's picture is right, the[n] the Gospel writers almost certain[ly] had contact with each other, an[d] tried deliberately to suppleme[nt] each other. This has long bee[n] recognized in the case of Mar[k.] Mark is the shortest Gospel, an[d] about 95% of his content i[s] reproduced in Matthew and Luk[e,] which are both much longer. [It] looks very much as if Mark was th[e]

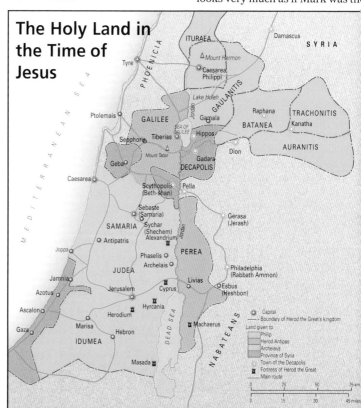

The Holy Land in the Time of Jesus

rst to be written, and then Matthew and Luke both used Mark, adding further extensive material. Scholars cannot decide whether Matthew knew Luke, or vice versa, or whether they were written independently. John has so little material in common with the others that it looks as if he knew all three, and deliberately tried to widen the picture they paint—using other traditions, and telling the story very differently.

So it seems as though the Gospel writers each knew that the other Gospels were inadequate, and sought to extend the picture. The first Christians recognized this by refusing to choose among them, and accepting all four together as providing a composite of Jesus of Nazareth.

How accurate is this composite?

The Gospels first circulated under the gaze of eyewitnesses of Jesus' ministry. Luke claims that his Gospel rests upon extensive research among "eyewitnesses and ministers of the Word"—that is (probably), those charged with remembering the "Word" of Jesus (Luke 1:1-4—see the scroll above). Within the parameters of the "*Bios*" genre, Luke strove for accuracy. The differences among the Gospels underline the impression of a figure of such towering significance that any attempt to capture Him in words is bound to be inadequate. But there is no need to doubt the broad reliability of these accounts.

Mark

An early tradition connects Mark's Gospel with Peter (see 1 Peter 5:13), and it is likely that Mark represents the collection of stories and traditions that Peter used in his long ministry. Mark wove them together into a crisp and vivid presentation of Jesus, emphasizing His power as a healer, His preaching (although

Outline of Mark

1:1-15	The scene is set
1:16–3:6	Jesus' initial ministry in Galilee
3:7–4:34	Jesus the Teacher
4:35–6:6	Jesus the Healer
6:7–9:1	On a wider stage: Jesus the Messiah?
9:2–10:45	The heart of discipleship: Jesus the Leader
10:46–13:37	Jesus the Son of David, the Master of the House
14:1–15:47	Jesus the new Covenant Sacrifice
16:1-8	The new start

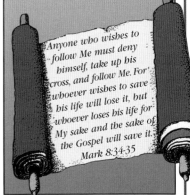

The Church of the Holy Sepulcher, Jerusalem, probable site of Jesus' death and burial.

Mark doesn't record much of it), the opposition He provoked, the puzzlement He caused even among His disciples, and their difficulty in deciding who or what He was. Mark emphasizes Jesus' expectation of His own death, His call to sacrificial discipleship embracing suffering like His, and His pronouncement of judgment on the Temple and the leaders of Israel. He tells the story of Jesus' last week in great detail. The Resurrection is not directly described, and Mark's story does not end so much as break off, as though Mark wanted to convey an impression of incompleteness.

Matthew

Matthew's Gospel is very different from Mark's, although he incorporates nearly the whole of Mark (about 92%). When he uses Mark's material, he usually condenses it, telling the stories with less detail (and thus less vividly). His Gospel is about 60% longer than Mark, with a wealth of new material.

Who wrote the first Gospel—and when?
The ascription to Matthew, one of Jesus' disciples (also called "Levi": Matthew 9:9; 10:3; Mark 2:14) goes back to the early second century, and there is little reason to doubt it. Many scholars propose that Mat-thew-Levi wrote part of this Gospel and another author (probably a converted Pharisee) completed it, adding much of its very Jewish tenor.

The second question is harder to answer. If Matthew borrowed from Mark, which seems to be the case, then Matthew (at least the final, enlarged version of the Gospel) was probably written around A.D. 80.

Why was Matthew written?
Matthew's Jewishness (his interest in the fulfillment of Scripture, for instance—see next page) has suggested to some that he was writing for Jewish Christians, perhaps fo a specific group troubled by difficult relationship with th synagogue. At first, most Jewis Christians continued to worship i their local synagogue. But as th first century progressed, rela tionships became increasingl strained, especially as the numbe of Gentile Christians multiplie and Jewish Christians felt mor and more pressure to live i fellowship with them. If they di so, they could no longer obey th traditional Jewish food and purit laws.

So in many places there cam a "parting of the ways," to us the understated phrase by whic scholars describe a painful sev ering of relationships betwee Jews and Christians. For instance the ways parted in Jerusalem whe the Jewish Christians there obeye Jesus' command in Matthew 24:15 16 and fled across the Jordan whe the Romans advanced to attack They did not stay to defen Jerusalem alongside their fellov Jews.

Prof. Graham Stanton of Cam bridge University suggests that th trauma surrounding this parting o the ways prompted Matthew to write for his group of churches. He

Cutaway illustration of the synagogue at Capernaum, probably built on the same site as the synagogue at which Jesus taught. The lectern from which the Scriptures were read is clearly visible.

Pharisee at prayer, with prayer shawl and phylacteries.

wanted to show how Jesus fulfills the Law (e.g., 5:17), how He too was rejected by His fellow Jews, how He criticized the Jewish leadership and especially accused them of wrongly interpreting the Law (chapters 5 and 23), and how He called His followers to respond with love toward their enemies (5:43ff.) and to reach out positively to the Gentile world in His Name (10:18; 28:18-20).

On the other hand, as we saw earlier, Richard Bauckham cautions us against finding local purposes for the Gospels. Such suggestions generally only relate to parts of the Gospel. So maybe we should give weight just to the comparison with Mark: Matthew simply wanted to enlarge Mark's picture of Jesus, especially by adding records of His actual teaching.

Matthew's special interests

Here is a summary of the four emphases that distinguish Matthew from the other Gospels:

• *The fulfillment of the Old Testament*. On twelve occasions Matthew notes that this or that took place "to fulfill the words of the prophet. . . ." In addition, he records Jesus' saying that "I have not come to abolish [the Law or the prophets] but to fulfill them" (5:17). The genealogy with which he begins emphasizes Jesus' position as "Son of David"—the Messiah who comes laden with Old Testament promise.

• *Jesus as Teacher*. Matthew includes five solid blocks of teaching from Jesus, most notably the "Sermon on the Mount" (chapters 5–7: also chapters 10, 13, 18, and 23–25). This probably reflects a concern with teaching and discipling new converts. Matthew wrote his Gospel so that the story has a kind of topical structure—see the panel to the right.

• *Outreach to the Gentile world*. The appearance in chapter 2 of the "wise men"—astrologers—from the East signals Matthew's conviction that this "King of the Jews" is set to rule the whole world. This conviction is given concrete shape at the other end of the Gospel, when Jesus claims authority over heaven and earth and commissions His disciples to "make disciples of all nations" (28:18-19). In between we meet significant individuals such as the Roman centurion whose faith is greater than that of any Jew (8:5-13), we see "the Son of Man" sitting on the throne to judge all nations (25:31ff.), and we hear Jesus' famous "mission discourse" (chapter 10).

• *Issues of Church peace and discipline*. Matthew's emphasis on practical discipleship shades over into a concern with conflict management and discipline within the Church. This appears especially in chapter 18 (where he alone uses the word "Church," 18:17, compare 16:18), but we can discern this interest in other passages also, like 5:21-26 and 7:1-5.

Outline of Matthew

1:1-17	Prologue: Jesus the bearer of Israel's promise
1:18–2:23	His birth, in fulfillment of prophecy
3:1–9:35	**Introducing the Son of God**
3:1–4:25	Attested, tested, and into action
5:1–7:29	The authority of His Word in His teaching
8:1–9:35	The authority of His Word in His healing
9:36–12:50	Following the Son of God: issues of discipleship
13:1–16:12	The King, the Kingdom, and the rulers of Israel
16:13–20:34	Confessing the Son of God: issues of self-giving and suffering
21:1–23:39	The Son of God and the past: issues of Scripture, people, and interpretation
24:1–25:46	The Son of God and the future: issues of judgment and salvation
26:1–28:20	The Son of God, crucified, risen, and Lord of all

*Have you understood all this?" He asked. They answered, "Yes." Then He said to them, "Therefore, every teacher of the law . . . is like the owner of a house who brings forth from his storeroom new treasures as well as old."
Matthew 13:51-52*

Matthew's interest in the Old Testament

A survey of Matthew's "fulfillment" passages conveys the strength of his concerns to show how the Old Testament was fulfilled through Jesus.
Matthew 1:22; 2:15; 2:17; 2:23; 4:14; 8:17; 12:17; 13:14; 13:35; 21:4; 26:56; 27:9

Luke

Luke's Gospel is the longest of the four—in fact, the longest single work in the New Testament. It forms a two-volume work with the Acts of the Apostles, ascribed to Paul's traveling companion Luke from the earliest years of the Church.

Luke also incorporates much of Mark's Gospel, but less than Matthew—about 55% of it, contributing about 30% of his material. But unlike Matthew, Luke has "bunched" the material he has in common with Mark: it appears (broadly) in chapters 5–6, 8–9, 18, and 19–22. In the middle of Luke's Gospel is a long section (9:51–18:14), which has no parallels in Mark, and not many in Matthew. It has been called Luke's Travel Narrative, for at the start of this section Jesus "set His sights on Jerusalem" (9:51), and from then onward is on the move, gradually traveling south from Galilee for the final showdown in Judea.

Luke's purpose

Luke himself refers to "many" who had produced written accounts of Jesus before him (1:1). In comparison with these "many," Luke sets out to produce "an orderly account" for his patron, Theophilus, based on his own careful research (1:3). He gives us the impression that confusion reigned supreme–prompting his desire to provide Theophilus with a definitive account (1:4).

Theophilus

Some have argued that Theophilus is a symbolic name for all Christians, for the meaning of his name is "lover of God." Or he could possibly have been real, perhaps a wealthy, newly converted (and confused?) Christian who supported Luke through his period of research. Maybe he lived in Caesarea Philippi, for it appears that Luke was with Paul for at least part of his two-year imprisonment there (Acts 27:1), and this would have been an excellent base from which to research the Gospel.

Luke with Acts

It is important to read the Gospel and Acts together, for they have many themes in common and an overarching structure that unites them. For instance, Luke's birth narrative (unique to him) contains the figure of Simeon, an old Jew "awaiting the consolation of Israel" (Luke 2:25), who recognizes the Baby Jesus as the Messiah and prophesies that He will bring salvation to "all the peoples, a light of revelation to the Gentiles and glory for Your people Israel" (2:31-32). This prophecy looks forward to the end of the Book of Acts,

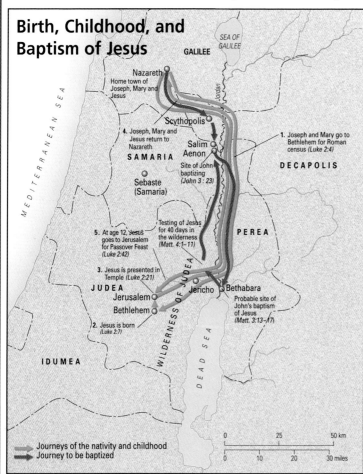

Birth, Childhood, and Baptism of Jesus

SEA OF GALILEE

GALILEE

MEDITERRANEAN SEA

Nazareth
Home town of Joseph, Mary and Jesus

Jordan

Scythopolis

4. Joseph, Mary and Jesus return to Nazareth

SAMARIA

Salim
Aenon

Site of John baptizing (John 3:23)

1. Joseph and Mary go to Bethlehem for Roman census (Luke 2:4)

DECAPOLIS

Sebaste (Samaria)

Testing of Jesus for 40 days in the wilderness (Matt. 4:1–11)

PEREA

5. At age 12, Jesus goes to Jerusalem for Passover Feast (Luke 2:42)

3. Jesus is presented in Temple (Luke 2:21)

JUDEA

Jerusalem

Bethlehem

Jericho

Bethabara
Probable site of John's baptism of Jesus (Matt. 3:13–17)

2. Jesus is born (Luke 2:7)

WILDERNESS OF JUDEA

IDUMEA

DEAD SEA

Journeys of the nativity and childhood
Journey to be baptized

0   25   50 km
0   10   20   30 miles

Luke's themes and interests

There are many, including:

• *The Holy Spirit.* Luke emphasizes the rebirth of prophecy at the time of Jesus' birth (e.g., 1:41; 1:67) and the power of the Spirit resting on Jesus (1:35; 3:22; 4:14); this anticipates his great interest in the Spirit in Acts.

• *Poverty and riches.* Much material signals Luke's interest in the deceptiveness of wealth, and the blessings of poverty, especially the voluntary poverty to which Jesus calls His disciples (e.g., 1:53; 6:20-26; 12:13-21; 14:33; 16:19-31; 19:1-10, etc.). This theme, too, is developed in Acts.

• *Women.* The prominent role played by women in the Acts story is anticipated in the Gospel as we see Jesus treating women very differently from the norm in Jewish culture: e.g., 7:36-50; 8:1-3. And Luke follows this through by emphasizing the female players: Mary, Elizabeth, Anna (2:36-38), the widow of Nain (7:11-17),

Martha and Mary (10:38-42), the "daughter of Abraham" bound by Satan (13:10-17—the only known occasion on which this female equivalent of "son of Abraham" is used).

• *Social outcasts.* Jesus' ministry to social outcasts is a feature in all the Gospels, but Luke takes special delight in it. Whether it's poor shepherds (2:8ff.), a rich tax collector (18:9-14; 19:1-10), a prodigal son (15:11-32), unclean Samaritans (10:29-37; 17:11-19), a prostitute (7:36-50), or a crucified thief (23:39-43), Luke loves to show the doors of the Kingdom being thrown wide for them.

• *Prayer.* Where his story runs parallel to Matthew and Mark, Luke adds a reference to prayer on no fewer than eleven occasions. He emphasizes Jesus' private prayer (5:16; 6:12; 9:18), especially at vital moments (3:21; 9:28), and makes His example inspiring (11:1), not to say awesome (22:40-46).

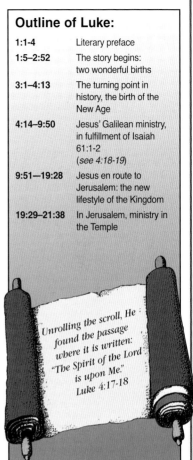

Unrolling the scroll, He found the passage where it is written: "The Spirit of the Lord is upon Me." Luke 4:17-18

Luke the physician, with the tools of his trade.

where the Gospel message has reached Rome, the center of the Empire, and we hear Paul's comment that "this salvation offered by God has been sent to the Gentiles" (Acts 28:28). Luke's message is that Israel finds her salvation and "glory" in and through the salvation of the Gentiles by faith in Christ, and not in rivalry or separation.

Luke probably wrote primarily for Gentile readers such as Theophilus. His Greek is cultured and vivid, although he deliberately employs the style of Septuagint (Old Testament) Greek in his opening chapters, to underline the Jewishness of the start of this powerful, well-told story.

John

"John last of all, conscious that the 'bodily' facts had been made clear in the [Synoptic] Gospels, was urged by his companions and, divinely moved by the Spirit, composed a 'spiritual' Gospel." These words come from the end of the second century, from the pen of Clement of Alexandria. And in modern scholarship Clement's description of John as "a spiritual Gospel" has seemed to summarize John's apparent interest in the meaning of Jesus' life, rather than in the facts of it. For instance, John includes long "discourses," unparalleled in the Synoptics, in which Jesus makes powerful and dramatic claims for Himself (e.g., 5:19-47; 6:35-58; 10:1-39). Whereas in the Synoptics Jesus is reluctant to call Himself "Messiah" or "Son of God" in public (e.g., Mark 8:29-30), He does not hesitate in John!

John's aim

But even a quick reading reveals that John is not unaware of a distinction between "the facts" and "the meaning." He includes hosts of narrative details, for instance, of time and place. It is he who gives us the tradition that Jesus' ministry lasted for over two years, including at least three Passovers. The Gospel presents itself as eyewitness testimony to the Incarnation of the Word (1:14). In this respect, John is no different from the Synoptics: as a "*Bios*," his Gospel aims to present the historical Jesus so that readers may understand Him.

John and the Synoptics

Why then is John so different from the Synoptics? This is a most important question—the credibility of the Gospels as reliable guides depends upon it. The earliest answer was given by second-century Gnostic Christians, who fell in love with John because it seemed to contain special, secret traditions of Jesus that supported their mystical approach to the faith. They believed that John had drawn on separate traditions, unknown or unused by the other evangelists.

This view of John was revived in the twentieth century, especially by Prof. C.H. Dodd, who argued that John wrote independently of the Synoptic Gospels, drawing on Jesus traditions associated with Judea rather than with Galilee. There may well be truth in this, but it is noteworthy that in John, even when Jesus is in Galilee, the stories barely coincide. John gives

Titus's Arch, Rome.

us the wedding at Cana (2:1-11), to which there is no Synoptic parallel; the royal official (4:46-54) which has some elements in common with the centurion story in Luke 7:1-10 but may be a different story altogether; and the feeding of the five thousand followed by the stilling of the storm, which occur together in Matthew and Mark as in John (Matthew 14:13-33; Mark 6:34-52; John 6:1-21), but which John expands with the "Bread of Life" discourse (6:22-59). John is aware of a wider ministry in Galilee (7:1), but seems deliberately to have used material not in the Synoptics.

A tiled cafe sign in modern Cana. John gives us the wedding at Cana (2:1-11), to which there is no Synoptic parallel.

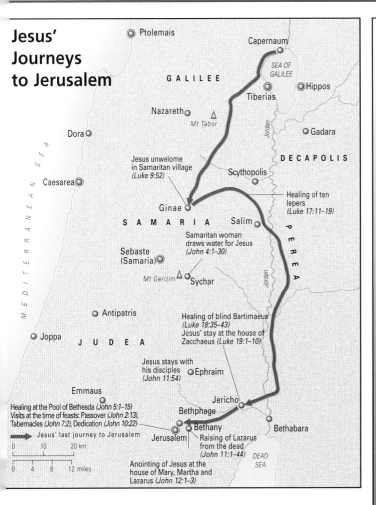

Jesus' Journeys to Jerusalem

Ptolemais

Capernaum

SEA OF GALILEE

GALILEE

Hippos

Tiberias

Nazareth

△ Mt Tabor

Dora

Gadara

DECAPOLIS

Jesus unwelome in Samaritan village (Luke 9:52)

Scythopolis

Caesarea

Healing of ten lepers (Luke 17:11–19)

Ginae

SAMARIA   Salim

P E R E A

Samaritan woman draws water for Jesus (John 4:1–30)

Sebaste (Samaria)

Mt Gerizim △ Sychar

Jordan

Antipatris

Healing of blind Bartimaeus (Luke 18:35–43)
Jesus' stay at the house of Zacchaeus (Luke 19:1–10)

Joppa   J U D E A

Jesus stays with his disciples (John 11:54)   Ephraim

Emmaus

Jericho

Healing at the Pool of Bethesda (John 5:1–15)
Visits at the time of feasts: Passover (John 2:13),
Tabernacles (John 7:2), Dedication (John 10:22)

Bethphage

Jesus' last journey to Jerusalem   Jerusalem   Bethany   Bethabara

0   10   20 km

0   4   8   12 miles

Raising of Lazarus from the dead (John 11:1–44)   DEAD SEA

Anointing of Jesus at the house of Mary, Martha and Lazarus (John 12:1–3)

M E D I T E R R A N E A N   S E A

An outline of John:

1:1-18	The Prologue: the Word of God becomes flesh
1:19–2:12	The Word revealed to Israel in the testimony of others
2:13–4:54	The Word revealed as Savior of Israel, Samaria—and the world (Passover)
5:1–6:71	The Word as the Giver of Life (Tabernacles, Passover)
7:1–10:21	The Word and human reaction: faith and dispute (Tabernacles)
10:22–11:54	The Word as the Restorer of Israel (Dedication)
11:55–13:30	The Word prepares for Passover, to lay down His life
13:31–17:26	The Word looks forward to the life of the Church
18:1–20:31	The death and Resurrection of the Word
21:1-25	The Word commissions the Church

But those written here have been recorded so that you may come to believe that Jesus is the Christ, the Son of God, and that through your belief you may have life in His Name.
John 20:31

Deliberately? This involves a subtle and balanced judgment. In light of what we know about the Jesus traditions in the early Church, is it more likely that John deliberately, or accidentally, ended up so different? The large amount of material in common among the Synoptics supports the view that the stories of Jesus' short ministry quickly became standardized around a fairly limited corpus of shared memories. And so the balance of probability tips toward the deliberate supplementation of the Synoptics by someone who was aware of much extra material not caught up into the Synoptic tradition. In particular, he used "controversy" material—traditions of Jesus' arguments with Jewish scholars in Jerusalem, in which He had been much more open about His claims than He usually was with the ordinary people.

John's readership

What governed John's choice? Recent scholarship has underlined his Jewishness—revealed in his interest in the Temple and the Jewish festivals (around which he structures the Gospel), in the Old Testament and its right interpretation, and in his use of "wisdom" ideas, of Moses traditions, of the "I am" sayings in Isaiah 40–55, and of the imagery of light, water, bread, and sheep associated with the Law and with Israel. While clearly directed at a wide audience—for instance, explaining Jewish cus-toms and terms for Gentile readers —it could well be that John wrote especially for Jews in the aftermath of the destruction of the Temple and Jerusalem in A.D. 70, wanting to present Jesus as the answer to their loss and their need.

Many recent writers, such as Prof. Alan Culpepper, have underlined the literary artistry of John's Gospel, its quality and power as a story. It retains this power across time and culture, one of the great classics of world literature.

The Acts of the Apostles

Luke's second volume, Acts, is the second longest document in the New Testament. Like his Gospel, it is structured around a journey. Parallel to Jesus' journey to Jerusalem is Paul's journey to Rome. Both journeys carry God's plan of salvation with them—salvation won at great personal cost (although, of course, Luke does not present Paul as a Savior like Jesus).

Paul's commission

At Paul's conversion, the Lord appoints him as "a vessel to bring My name before the Gentiles and their kings and before the people of Israel" (9:15). He becomes the center of the story from chapter 13 onward, as we see the Gospel spreading westward through Paul's ministry, until he reaches Rome (as a prisoner) in chapter 28. But Israel is never forgotten— throughout the story Paul's priority is to contact Jews first. But Luke's great passion is to display the universal relevance and power of the Gospel, as foreshadowed at the start of the story, in Acts 1:8.

Luke's participation

Luke himself becomes a participant in the second half of the book. In 16:10, in the middle of Paul's second missionary journey, a "we" suddenly appears in the narrative, and the author apparently accompanies Paul on the following journey to Philippi. The "we" ceases when Paul leaves Philippi (16:40), only to reappear when Paul returns there in 20:5. The author then accompanies Paul to Jerusalem (21:17), disappears during the events related in chapters 22–26, but reappears for Paul's final journey to Rome (27:1–28:16).

The author thus subtly gives us confidence in the reliability of the

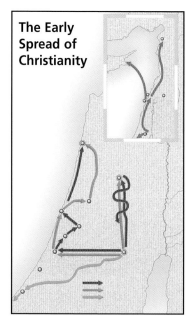

The Early Spread of Christianity

narrative. It is clear, for instance, that he took great pains to note the details of the sea journey and shipwreck in Acts 27 (one of the "we" passages). Because this fits so well with his comment in Luke 1:3 about careful research, we gain confidence in the whole story.

Relief on a Roman gravestone, Philippi, scene of Paul's imprisonment (Acts 17).

Luke's purpose

But Luke was writing as an ancient, not a modern, historian. So he does not provide answers to some of the questions that interest us. What, for instance, happened to the other Apostles listed in Acts 1:13? How many of the 3,000 converted at Pentecost were from the places listed in 2:9? Did they then establish churches "back home"? How did the Gospel spread east from Jerusalem? What in fact were the dates of the landmark events—Paul's conversion, the murder of James, the Apostolic Council? Asking questions like these reveals that Luke's purpose was not to provide an overall survey of the first three decades of Church history, but to give a demonstration of the power and potential of the Gospel in action, and of its growth from Jewish infant to worldwide adolescent.

Built into the story—and arising from this purpose—are various theological issues, discussion of which Luke skillfully weaves into his narrative. We pick out three:

• *Church growth and the plan of God.* Luke wanted to show God at work through the story, because he believed that the Gospel was God's means of salvation for all (4:12). But at the same time he had a very human story to tell, including many mistakes, disagreements, and setbacks. On the one hand, God had already appointed "the dates or the times" by which the Kingdom would come (1:7), so that the growth of the Church was inevitable and irresistible (5:38-39). But on the other hand, the Gospel encountered strong opposition, and that opposition was actually essential to the story, because Jesus' Crucifixion had been both God's plan and an act of

ASIA
Pergamum
Sardis
Ephesus
Miletus
PHRYGIA
GALATIA
PISIDIA
Antioch
LYCAONIA
Iconium
Derbe
Lystra
CILICIA
Tarsus
PAMPHYLIA
Attalia
Perga
Seleucia
Antioch
Myra
Rhodes
RHODES
CYPRUS
Salamis
Paphos
SYRIA
3. Paul and Barnabas are mistaken for gods after Paul's healing of a lame man (Acts 14:8-13)
1. Paul and Barnabas set sail for Cyprus
2. Elymas the sorcerer
MEDITERRANEAN SEA
Caesarea
Jerusalem
EGYPT
0 125 250 km
0 50 100 150 miles
Area of Jewish settlement

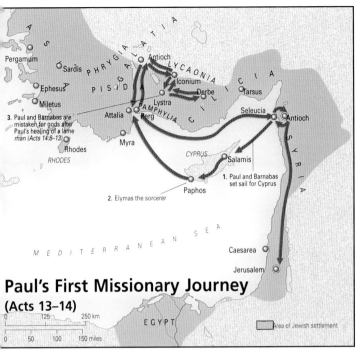

Paul's First Missionary Journey (Acts 13–14)

Outline of Acts

1:1–2:47	The story begins: all God's people receive the Spirit
3:1–4:37	The Spirit-filled life: power, boldness, prayer, fellowship
5:1–8:3	Opposition in Jerusalem: the Empire strikes back
8:4–11:18	Victory through defeat: the secret of Church growth
11:19–14:28	Bursting out: the Antioch church moves into mission
15:1-35	Controversy within: Jews and Gentiles in the Church
15:36–18:22	Paul's second mission from Antioch
18:23–21:16	Off again: from Antioch to Jerusalem via Greece
21:17–26:32	Paul in prison and on trial
27:1–28:31	And so to Rome: the Gospel at the heart of the Empire

readful wickedness (see 2:23; :13-15; 4:10).

So Luke shows God thoroughly ıvolved in a messy story, preparing Saul even as Stephen is toned, releasing Peter from prison after James's death, bringing ;ood out of Paul and Barnabas's rgument, and getting the Gospel

Paul's Conversion
Tarsus
4. The apostles send Paul to Tarsus for his safety
Antioch
Seleucia
SYRIA
CYPRUS
MEDITERRANEAN SEA
PHOENICIA
2. Ananias baptizes Paul (Acts 9:10-19)
Damascus
Sidon
Tyre
3. Paul preaches Christianity and Hellenists threaten to kill him
KINGDOM OF HEROD AGRIPPA I
Jordan
1. Paul sees vision of Christ on the road to Damascus
Caesarea
Sebaste (Samaria)
Lydda
Jericho
Jerusalem
Dead Sea
0 50 100 km
0 20 40 60 miles

to Rome, but by a most tortuous and difficult route. Having been stoned at Lystra, Paul tells the Christians there, "It is necessary for us to undergo many hardships in order to enter the Kingdom of God" (14:22: for Luke, "necessary" points to God's plan).

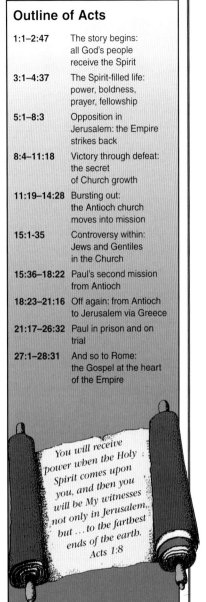

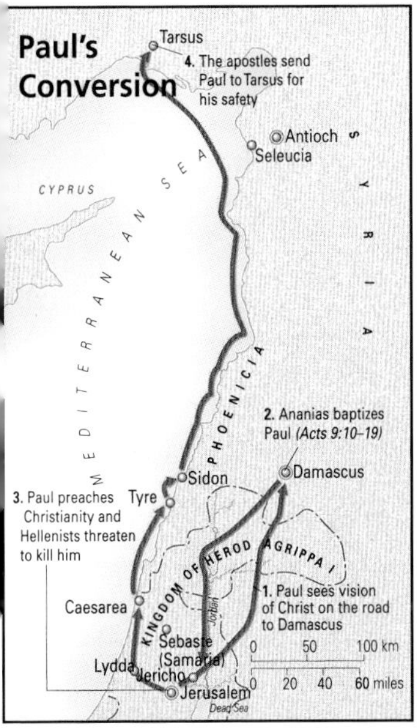

- *The relation between Jews and Gentiles before God.* The Gospel starts life Jewish. But must Gentiles become Jews in order to benefit from it? Luke shows the Christians wrestling with this, and his own answer is clear: certainly not! He follows the first Jewish Pentecost (chapter 2) with another in Samaria (chapter 8) and another for Gentiles (chapter 10), thus showing that the Spirit treats all equally.
- *The fulfillment of prophecy.* Luke is describing something completely new in the history of Israel. Never since the election of Abraham has anything happened like this. So he is eager to show that these events are not novel, as well as new, but are the proper fulfillment of Israel's covenant with God. He makes this case chiefly in the speeches that are

You will receive power when the Holy Spirit comes upon you, and then you will be My witnesses not only in Jerusalem, but . . . to the farthest ends of the earth.
Acts 1:8

such an important feature of Acts: see 2:16-36; 3:21-23; 4:11; 7:2-53; 8:32-35; 13:16-47; 15:13-21; 28:25-28. This has to be a powerful and essential case, if Jews and Gentiles alike are to be convinced.

Paul's Early Letters

The date of Galatians
The dating of Paul's letters is uncertain, and the date of Galatians particularly so. Galatians may not be one of "Paul's Early Letters." However, on balance, it is *probably* his earliest surviving letter, written to the churches he visited on his first missionary journey (Acts 13–14), during the period mentioned in Acts 15:35.

Faith or Law?
We learn much about Paul, and what made him tick, from Galatians. He was deeply concerned that his converts were abandoning "the Gospel of Christ" (1:7) by agreeing to be circumcised—under pressure from "the circumcised" (2:12). These were Jewish Christians like those referred to in Acts 15:1, who taught (as summarized there): "Unless you are circumcised in accordance with the tradition of Moses, you cannot be saved." They seem to have followed Paul around his new Galatian churches, adding this requirement to the Gospel that he had taught.

Paul was furious! "You foolish Galatians! Who has bewitched you?" (3:1). Passionately he argues that circumcision is a sign of a wholly different kind of relationship with God—a relationship based on Law and requirement, rather than on faith and grace (3:11-12; 5:3-6). His own experience on the Damascus Road is vital here (1:13-16): at that moment he "died to the Law" (2:19), for he discovered, to his horror, that in his zeal for the Law he "persecuted the Church of God" (1:13). And since the Messiah had to die, the Law could not be God's answer to sin, as he had thought: "If justification comes through the Law, Christ died for nothing" (2:21, cf. 3:21ff.).

So the thought that his Galatians might turn to the Law for salvation felt to Paul like rejecting Christ and joining His enemies. He recounts how he stood out in public against Peter himself, when the latter "wobbled" under pressure from "the circumcised" (2:11-16). How did you receive the Spirit? he pointedly asks the Galatians: by obeying the law, or by believing in Jesus? (3:2).

1 & 2 Thessalonians
1 Thessalonians is probably Paul's second letter—written from Athens, not long after the campaign in Thessalonica recorded in Acts 17:1-10. 2 Thessalonians followed, probably within months. Many scholars believe that 2 Thessalonians is not by Paul, because of its different teaching about the Second Coming of Christ (compare 1 Thessalonians 4:13–5:11 with 2 Thessalonians 2:1-12). But Paul is tackling different problems in the two letters, and drawing on different aspects of his teaching to do so. In the first letter he deals with the Thessalonians' concern about the premature death of some believers; in the second, with the strange view that the *"parousia"* (Second Coming) of Christ had already occurred.

Opposition in Thessalonica
The Gospel met immediate opposition in Thessalonica. Some of the first Jewish converts were grabbed by a rioting crowd and dragged before the city authorities, charged with sedition against Rome. Paul and Silas had to escape from the city under cover of night.

What caused this opposition? It is clear that first Paul himself, and then his Thessalonian converts, felt the sting of the same passionate persecution that he himself had launched at the Church. The

We know that a man is justified not by the works of the Law but through faith in Jesus Christ.
Galatians 2:16

Fact file: Paul

34 A.D.	Converted on the Damascus Road
37	First visit to Jerusalem (*Galatians 1:18, Acts 9:26-30*). Returns to Tarsus
47-48	Ministers in Antioch (*Acts 11:25-26*)
48	Second visit to Jerusalem (*Galatians 2:1-10; Acts 11:30*)
49	First missionary journey–to the Galatian churches (*Acts 13–14*)
49	Apostolic Council in Jerusalem (*Acts 15*)
50	Writes Galatians. Second missionary journey begins (*Acts 15:36*). Ministers in Thessalonica, arrives in Corinth (*Acts 18:1*)
50-51	Writes 1 and 2 Thessalonians

Paul's Second Missionary Journey

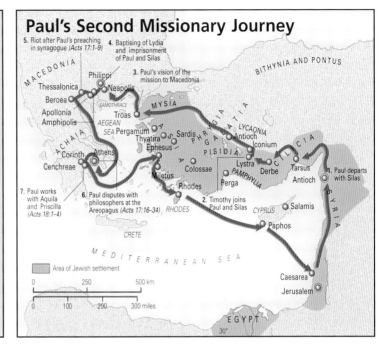

reasons may have been different, but the fundamental motivation was the same: "zeal for the Law."

Why Paul provoked such hatred we can see, for instance, in 1 Thessalonians 1:4-5. Paul calls the Thessalonians "brethren beloved by God," and says "we know that He has chosen you, because our Gospel came to you . . . in power."

The terms "beloved" and "chosen" are both technical terms, special to Israel's relationship with God. Paul applies them without hesitation to these Gentile Thessalonians because he really believed, as he says in Galatians 3:28-29, that the old covenant distinction between Israel and the Gentiles had been abolished, and Gentiles had become "the offspring of Abraham" through faith in Christ. Similarly in 1 Thessalonians 2:13 Paul insists that his message is "the Word of God" —a description that ought to be reserved for the Sacred Scriptures of Israel! No wonder the "zealous for the Law" tried to stop him. They could not accept such a denial of Israel's special status.

Paul—missionary pastor

These three letters give us unique insight into Paul the missionary, pastor, and theologian. He felt commissioned by God Himself to preach a unique Gospel, which he believed he had received directly from Christ on the Damascus Road (Galatians 1:12). But if Galatians makes him seem rather fierce, 1 Thessalonians is full of moving expressions of love and concern for his converts. And in both the Thessalonian letters we see the motivating conviction behind his missionary zeal—the belief that Christ would return soon as Savior and Judge of all.

Remains of the Roman aqueduct at Antioch, Asia Minor.

Paul and Corinth

Paul's two letters to the church at Corinth provide powerful insight into Paul the person, and into his teaching on a wide range of topics: not just the big "theological" topics like Christ, the Law, the Cross and atonement, the Holy Spirit, Resurrection, and final judgment, but also many practical issues such as Church discipline, sex and marriage, relation to pagan society, the Eucharist, the use of "spiritual gifts," love and unity, giving, and attitudes toward suffering. Woven into this great mix is the constant thread of Paul's own relationship with the church in Corinth.

Conflict in Corinth

The opposition seems to have started soon after Paul left Corinth. He had ministered there for eighteen months or more (Acts 18:11, 18), before returning to his home church in Antioch. But soon he was off again—his third missionary journey—and before long settled in Ephesus for a ministry of over two years (Acts 19:8, 10). 1 Corinthians was probably written in his second year there (1 Corinthians 16:8-9). But by then he had already written to the church at least once, for in 1 Corinthians 5:9-11 he refers to an earlier letter that they had misunderstood.

2 Corinthians was written with much emotion from Macedonia (Acts 20:1; 2 Corinthians 7:5). Paul had left Ephesus and traveled north, deciding not to visit Corinth, because an earlier visit (not recorded in Acts) had been so "painful," both to him and to the Corinthians (2:1; 13:2). Instead, he had written "with great distress and anguish of heart" (2:4), and then waited anxiously for Titus to return with their reply. Eventually Titus met Paul in Macedonia with good news (7:7-16). In response, Paul dashed off 2 Corinthians, vivid, passionate, disorganized (so much so that some scholars propose that it is actually fragments of three letters—the "first" letter, the "angry" letter, and a "reconciliation" letter

Remains of the ancient Temple of Apollo, Corinth.

pasted together), sparkling in style and in theology—his most personal and revealing letter.

Troubles in the church

What was the problem? In 1 Corinthians Paul compiles a sad catalog, although he pointedly starts with warm encouragement (1:4-9). There was grave immorality, which for some reason they were happy to accept (5:1-2). Some of the wealthier Christians had been taking each other to court over grievances (6:1-8). Some church members had been using prostitutes, while others had been renouncing sex altogether, even within marriage (6:12-20; 7:1ff.). There was also disagreement—and hurt consciences—over whether it was right to eat meat that had been offered in temples and then sold in the market (chapters 8–10). Paul was deeply concerned about their worship services, especially the conduct of some women (11:2-16), the divisions between rich and poor apparent at the Eucharist (11:17-34), and their overuse of the gift of tongues (chapter 14). If this were not bad enough, the church had divided into factions claiming favorite teachers (1:12), and some were denying the bodily Resurrection of Christ (15:12).

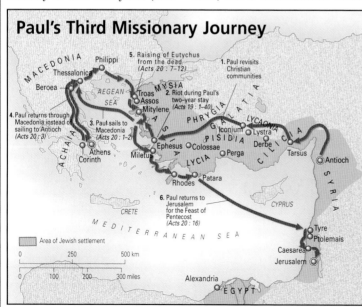

Paul's Third Missionary Journey

5. Raising of Eutychus from the dead (Acts 20 : 7-12)

1. Paul revisits Christian communities

2. Riot during Paul's two-year stay (Acts 19 : 1-40)

3. Paul sails to Macedonia (Acts 20 : 1-2)

4. Paul returns through Macedonia instead of sailing to Antioch (Acts 20 : 3)

6. Paul returns to Jerusalem for the Feast of Pentecost (Acts 20 : 16)

MACEDONIA — Philippi, Thessalonica, Beroea

AEGEAN SEA

MYSIA — Troas, Assos, Mitylene

PHRYGIA

GALATIA — Iconium, Lystra, Derbe

LYCAONIA

PISIDIA

Ephesus, Colossae, Perga

Miletus

ACHAIA — Athens, Corinth

LYCIA

CILICIA — Tarsus

Antioch

Rhodes, Patara

CRETE

CYPRUS

SYRIA

MEDITERRANEAN SEA

Tyre, Ptolemais

Caesarea, Jerusalem

Alexandria

EGYPT

Area of Jewish settlement

0   250   500 km

0 100 200 300 miles

Attacks on Paul

By the time we get to 2 Corinthians, Paul is aware of accusations made against him personally: that he lacks the decisiveness expected of a Spirit-filled person (1:15-22); that he does not have "letters of recommendation" from other churches (3:1-3); that he is a poor and unimpressive speaker (10:1, 10); that he cannot produce a proper list of miracles and visions to qualify as a true Apostle (12:10-12, cf. 1 Corinthians 4:8-13); that he pretended not to receive money from them but was actually feathering his own nest (12:14-18).

Paul's patience and love in the face of all this is truly moving, and deeply instructive for our understanding of him as a person and the conduct of his Apostleship. He does not mince his words, yet leaves the Corinthians in no doubt about his concern and care for them.

The source of the problems

Paul tackles the problems theologically—that is, by taking his readers back to the fundamental principles about Christ, the Church, the body, and the end of the world offended by their behavior. This reveals that the range of problems in Corinth may have had a common basis. Some were claiming to be "wise" (1 Corinthians 3:18), to have "knowledge" (1 Corinthians 8:1), to be "rich" (1 Corinthians 4:8, cf. 2 Corinthians 8:9) and "spiritual" (1 Corinthians 3:1). They spoke in angelic tongues (1 Corinthians 13:1), performed miracles, and believed that they had already experienced the Resurrection. ("There is no resurrection" in 1 Corinthians 15:12 means "there is no future bodily resurrection.") As "spiritual," they discounted the significance of the body—and so either indulged it with prostitutes or renounced sex completely, and had no objections to eating meat sacrificed to idols. "All things are lawful" was their slogan (1 Corinthians 6:12). Thinking about themselves in this way, it was easy to make distinctions

between themselves and the less "wise," and thus to create factions in the church.

Correcting the errors

Paul affirms their spiritual enthusiasm and experience, but not their arrogance or bad theology. He insists that Christ rose from the dead physically; that our resurrection is also physical, and future; that our bodies are spiritually significant as "limbs of Christ," that the "wise" and the "spiritual" do not divide into factions; that the Church is a unity as the Body of Christ, indwelt as a whole by the liberating Spirit of God; that he himself was appointed by God to bring the Gospel to Corinth; that weakness and suffering (rather than supercharged victory) are the norms for the Christian life, . . . etc., etc.! The richness of these two letters cannot adequately be summarized.

Who is weak, and I am not similarly afflicted? Who is led into sinfulness, and I am not filled with indignation?
2 Corinthians 11:29

Paul and Rome

Fact file: Paul

56	Writes to Rome from Corinth. Travels to Jerusalem. Riot, arrest, and hearing before Felix (*Acts 20–24*)
56-58	In prison without trial in Caesarea (*Acts 24:27*)
58	Hearings before Festus and Agrippa (*Acts 25–26*). Sea journey and shipwreck on Malta (*Acts 27:1–28:10*)
59	Arrives in Rome

Paul's letter to the Romans is his longest and most influential. Romans contains the clearest exposition of Paul's doctrine of justification by faith. Whereas Paul's other letters are related to problems in the churches addressed, Romans is more like a detached summary of his Gospel (1:16), perhaps sent to Rome because he wanted to introduce himself to them, so that they would willingly support him (1:13; 15:22-24).

Paul's manifesto

However, Romans is not "the Gospel in abstract." It is rooted in Paul's missionary work. Günther Bornkamm has called it "Paul's Last Will and Testament," because he suggests that Paul wrote it consciously at a turning point in his life. After finishing his ministry in the east (15:19, 23), he is now undertaking a dangerous journey to Jerusalem. He does not know whether he will survive it (15:30-31). So he sends to the Roman church, which he hopes to visit, a summary of the Gospel for which he has fought, "the power of God that offers salvation" for Jews and Gentiles alike (1:16) (possibly hoping that they will share this knowledge with the church in Jerusalem by whom their church was founded).

There is much drama, therefore, just under the surface. We catch echoes of the arguments, sometimes intense, through which Paul has come. And "justification by faith" is at the heart of it. In Galatians Paul argues his case directly and passionately. In Romans he reflects on the argument, draws wider implications, and spells out the consequences—but still passionately.

Justification by faith

The essence of the argument concerns the relation between Christ and God's covenant with Israel. For many Jewish Christians, the covenant was the foundation of all relationship with God. It was "forever"—enshrined in the promises given to Abraham and sealed by the giving of the Law through Moses. It followed, therefore, that the blessings brought by the Messiah were available only within the covenant—to Jews, first and foremost, but also to Gentiles who committed themselves to the

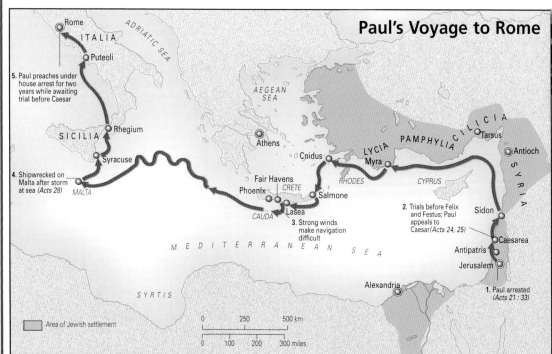

Paul's Voyage to Rome

- **5. Paul preaches under house arrest for two years while awaiting trial before Caesar**
- **4. Shipwrecked on Malta after storm at sea** (*Acts 28*)
- **3. Strong winds make navigation difficult**
- **2. Trials before Felix and Festus; Paul appeals to Caesar** (*Acts 24, 25*)
- **1. Paul arrested** (*Acts 21 : 33*)

Rome, ITALIA, Puteoli, ADRIATIC SEA, SICILIA, Rhegium, Syracuse, MALTA, AEGEAN SEA, Athens, Cnidus, Fair Havens, Phoenix, CRETE, Lasea, CAUDA, Salmone, RHODES, LYCIA, Myra, PAMPHYLIA, CILICIA, Tarsus, Antioch, CYPRUS, SYRIA, Sidon, Caesarea, Antipatris, Jerusalem, Alexandria, MEDITERRANEAN SEA, SYRTIS

Area of Jewish settlement

0 250 500 km
0 100 200 300 miles

The Forum, ancient Rome.

God of Israel through circumcision.

Paul's answer

Paul refused to accept this impressive argument. In a nutshell, he says:

1. The covenant with Israel was never designed to bring blessing exclusively to those within it, but was meant to bring blessing to the Gentile world. Paul uses Old Testament quotations to make this point (2:22-24; 4:16-17; 9:25-26; 10:12-13, 20; 15:8-12).

2. Neither was the covenant ever a guarantee of salvation. In fact, it promised judgment on the disobedient, as much as blessing on the circumcised (2:25-29; 9:27-29; 11:7-10, 20). Only Christ brings a guarantee of salvation (8:31-39), and He came not just to fulfill the promises to Abraham, but to meet the need of the world caused by the sin of Adam (5:12-21).

3. Jesus brings salvation, through His atoning death, to all who believe, Jew or Gentile (3:21-31), because all have exactly the same need of deliverance from the power of sin (1:18-32; 3:9-20).

4. Abraham was not "justified" before he was circumcised, and thus gives a pattern for today: uncircumcised Gentiles may be justified like him, and so claim him as their "father" (4:1-25).

5. And this has been Paul's experience: it is simply a fact that Gentile believers have received righteousness by faith in Christ—and this fact must revolutionize our understanding of the ways of God (2:14-16, 26-29; 3:22-24, 29-30; 9:30; 11:17). By the Holy Spirit, they have been transformed (6:17-18; 7:6; 8:9-10).

6. So life in the Spirit, rather than obedience to the Law, is what God now asks of His people. In any case, because of the power of sin, the Law could not deliver what it promised (7:4–8:8).

7. But God has not abandoned Israel! He is still faithful to His covenant promises. But these promises will be fulfilled in the context of the worldwide salvation that He plans (11:1-36).

8. So the Church, made up of Jews and Gentiles together and defined not by loyalty to Moses but by the love of Christ, is the body that can now rightly claim to be the people of God, and must live as such (12:1–15:13)!

An example to be heeded

It appears from chapter 14 that Paul probably also had a particular issue in mind—a conflict in the Roman church between Jewish and Gentile believers over practical issues arising from their life together—the observation of Jewish food laws and festivals. Amazingly, though he has argued strongly that "Christ is the fulfillment of the Law" (10:4), Paul gently encourages the Gentile Christians simply to accept their Jewish brothers and sisters, and not to require them to go against their consciences (14:13-23).

Bust of the Emperor Nero.

Paul's Later Letters

The New Testament contains a string of seven shorter letters from Paul: Philippians, Ephesians, Colossians, Philemon, and the "Pastoral" letters (1 and 2 Timothy, and Titus). All of these (except possibly Philippians) date from the last few years of Paul's life.

Authorship
Ephesians, Colossians, and the Pastorals are all regarded by some as "pseudonymous"—that is, written by disciples of Paul and published in his name after his death. This was not an uncommon practice, and in 2 Thessalonians 2:2 Paul expresses the fear that it may have already happened during his lifetime. The argument against this theory is that the early Church disapproved of it, because the authority of the Apostles was unique. Furthermore, it seems that Paul's letters were collected at a very early date (Paul himself encourages the process, in Colossians 4:16), when it would have been clear whether they were genuine or not.

Differences
If the later letters are all by Paul, then we are faced with the challenge of explaining the differences between them and his earlier letters. For instance, in Ephesians and Colossians he presents the Resurrection as something past (Ephesians 2:5-6; Colossians 3:1); in a way, that looks like the view he attacks in 1 Corinthians. The Greek style of the Pastorals is rather different, the great doctrine of justification by faith does not appear, and indeed "faith" has a different meaning—signifying the faith, the body of truths that Christians believe (e.g., 1 Timothy 3:9, 2 Timothy 3:8). Maybe this was due to developments in Paul's thinking or vocabulary, or by the different needs being addressed in these later letters, or by subtleties of thought that unite apparent differences.

Prison letters
Paul was in prison when writing all of the later letters except 1 Timothy and Titus. Which imprisonment is this? Acts mentions two (in Caesarea and in Rome), and Paul refers to "far more" imprisonments (2 Corinthians 11:23). The best suggestion is that

Stone relief of a Roman soldier.

all except 2 Timothy were written from the Acts 28 Roman imprisonment, and 2 Timothy from a later imprisonment in Rome, immediately prior to Paul's execution.

The view that Paul was released at the end of Acts 28 rests (a) on the tradition that he was martyred in the persecution by Nero in A.D. 65, and (b) on the references in the Pastorals to various movements by him around the Mediterranean, which cannot be fitted into the Acts narrative.

These marvelous letters are goldmines of teaching and encouragement.

Philippians
This is a thank-you letter, written to acknowledge the church's gift to him (2:25, 4:18). But Paul fills it out into a powerful discourse on facing suffering and death, turning the example of Christ into a pattern for the Christian life (1:18-30; 2:5-11). He writes movingly of the way that pattern has been written into his own experience (3:4-14), and warns against people who dress up worldly ambition as religion (3:17-21).

Ephesians and Colossians
These letters have much in common, and were clearly written at the same time. Ephesians may have been a circular letter, sent to several congregations in the

Remains of the prison at Philippi, dating from ancient times.

Remains of the massive theater at Ephesus, site of the riot caused by Paul's visit.

Fact file: Paul

59-61	Under house arrest in Rome (*Acts 28:30*). Writes Philippians, Ephesians, Colossians, and Philemon
61	Charges dropped and released?
61-64	Ministers again, possibly in Spain (*Romans 15:24*), Asia Minor (*Philemon 22, 2 Timothy 4:13*), Crete (*Titus 1:5*), Corinth (*2 Timothy 4:20*), Ephesus and Macedonia (*1 Timothy 1:3, 2 Timothy 1:18*). Writes 1 Timothy and Titus
64-65	Rearrested, tried, and executed in Rome (*2 Timothy 4:6,16*). Writes 2 Timothy

Ephesus area, for Paul is aware that many of the recipients will not know him now (Ephesians 3:2-4). Ephesians compares with Romans for its power and intensity: Paul focuses on the person of Christ, and displays His cosmic rule as the center of God's world plan. In Colossians he applies this cosmic picture of Christ to some of the religious conflicts his readers were facing.

Philemon

This letter is a little gem: by a huge coincidence, Paul came into contact, in Rome, with a slave who had run away from his master in the Lycus valley, 1,000 miles away—and the master turned out to be an old convert of Paul's. Through Paul Onesimus became a Christian, too—and now goes back to his master, Philemon, with this beautiful note entreating forgiveness and acceptance "no longer as a slave, but as more than a slave: as a brother" (verse 16). This letter speaks volumes about Paul's attitude to slavery. Clearly he felt that it was incompatible with Christian fellowship that brothers in Christ should also be masters and slaves. But he never attacked slavery as such, preferring to let the Gospel make its own appeal.

The Pastoral Letters

These letters probably date from a few years later. Timothy and Titus have been coworkers with Paul for about fifteen years, and have become leaders of stature in their own right. Paul has left them in charge in Ephesus and Crete, respectively, to appoint elders and deacons, to teach and to encourage and lead the churches. In addition, Timothy faced some tricky situations in Ephesus. The Pastorals are thus full of practical advice about Church leadership. 2 Timothy contains Paul's moving testimony in the face of imminent death.

An artist's impression of the Apostle Paul writing from his prison cell.

Hebrews

The letter to the Hebrews is an enigma. An enormously powerful piece of early Christian theology, clearly the product of a great and original mind—yet we do not know who wrote it, or to whom, or when, or where, or indeed why.

Is it a letter?

The first puzzle concerns its genre. Is it a letter, or a treatise? It has no opening greetings, but it ends like a letter (13:18-25). The style and contents have much in common with the treatises of Philo, the first-century Jewish philosopher, and yet we gather that the author is addressing a particular group of people (e.g., 5:11-12; 10:32-34). The best solution is that the original letter opening has been lost, which would have given us the author's and recipients' identity.

Who wrote Hebrews?

For many years Hebrews was ascribed to Paul, but this is impossible in the light of Hebrews 2:3-4. Here the author describes himself (or herself) as a second-generation Christian, which Paul refused to do (Galatians 1:12-17). Of the many suggestions, the most compelling is that it was written by Apollos, Paul's coworker in Corinth (1 Corinthians 3:4-7), who came from Alexandria and is described in Acts 18:24 as "an eloquent speaker" and "well-versed in the Scriptures." His origin in Alexandria could explain the parallels with Philo, who also came from there, and the author of Hebrews was certainly "well versed in the Scriptures"—see Acts 18:28.

The readers

Hebrews 13:24 possibly provides a clue about the recipients. "Those from Italy send you their greetings" suggests that they are in Italy, being greeted by their fellow countrymen who are with the author outside Italy. If so, Rome would be the best bet. More broadly, they are clearly Jewish Christians who seem to form a distinct community, with their own history (6:10; 10:32-34; 12:4) and leaders (13:17). This would have been possible in Rome, where the church was divided into several house-churches (Romans 16:5, 14-15).

Identity problems

For such Jewish-Christian groups, identity was a great problem. Where did they belong? Many still felt a strong loyalty to the synagogue, and yet the more they had fellowship with Gentiles, the more difficult their relationship with the synagogue became. If they ate with Gentiles, they would be branded law-breakers—and eventually apostates, if they persisted or deliberately broke off from the synagogue. Either way, they would lose their Jewishness. There seemed to be no cultural and religious middle ground.

The recipients of Hebrews are such a group! The author is clearly very concerned about them. The letter is peppered with warnings—not to "ignore" their salvation (2:3), "forsake" (3:12), "have fallen short" (4:1), "have fallen away" (6:6), "drawn back" (10:39); and with corresponding exhortations to "pay much closer attention" (2:1), "hold firm" (3:6), "make every effort" (4:11), "show the same diligence" (6:11), "approach with sincerity of heart" (10:22; 4:16). These verbs illustrate the pastoral tone of the whole letter.

Artist's impression of the Jewish High Priest in his full regalia.

The Tabernacle

The author of the Book of Hebrews assumes that his readers are well acquainted with the design of the Tabernacle. It was divided into two compartments. The first and larger was the "Holy Place." The further and smaller was the "Most Holy Place," the inner sanctuary. Here stood the ark, surmounted by its golden lid, the mercy seat, where the Shekinah glory, the visible symbol of God's presence, appeared.

The two "Places" were separated by a thick curtain called the veil. By this arrangement the Holy One of Israel was teaching His people both His presence among them, and His inaccessibility to them. He was near and yet far; sinners could draw near, but were not permitted to penetrate into His holy presence beyond the veil. Access to God was limited by four conditions, listed in Hebrews 9:7: *only the High Priest* might enter the inner sanctuary; but *only once a year* (on the Day of Atonement), *and only taking sacrificial blood* with him, to sprinkle on the mercy seat; and then he would secure remission *only for certain sins* (sins "committed in ignorance").

For our author, these limitations showed that "the way into the sanctuary had not been disclosed" (9:8); once again, the Old Testament reveals its own inadequacy and its need of Jesus. In contrast to the old High Priest, Jesus has "entered once for all into the sanctuary . . . with His Blood, thus obtaining eternal redemption" (9:12).

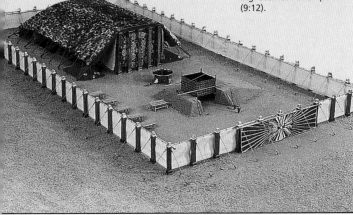

What was going on? Two theories have been proposed. Perhaps the recipients were so confused about their identity—Jewish or Christian?—that they were simply not making the progress in their faith that the author desires. He calls them "slow in learning" and "sluggish" in 5:11 and 6:12. Alternatively, he may have heard that they were actually abandoning their Christian commitment in order to stay in fellowship with the synagogue. 10:25 reads like a mild encouragement to church attendance: "Do not neglect to attend your assemblies, as some do . . ."—but we need to read this against the background sketched above, where meeting with Gentiles seriously compromises Jewish identity.

Jesus or Judaism?

Either way, the author's strategy is clear: he presents Jesus as the fulfillment of the Scriptures to the extent that without Jesus the Scriptures are left without coherent meaning.

The argument is deep and complex, and highly polemical. Hebrews argues that Christianity has replaced the old forms. The author seeks to claim the Old Testament for Christ, and Christ alone, arguing that, on its own, Israel's covenant with God is "aging [and] will shortly disappear" (8:13).

Peter and John

The Apostles Peter and John are often linked in the early stories in Acts (3:1; 4:13; 8:14), building on their association in Jesus' inner circle (Mark 5:37; 9:2; 13:3). So it is fitting that the New Testament should include letters from them both, written (probably) when both were in old age, Peter in Rome and John in Ephesus.

1 Peter

The ascription of these letters—two to Peter and three to John—is widely disputed. (We will look at 2 Peter beginning on page 28.) 1 Peter is written in good, lively, idiomatic Greek: is it possible that a Galilean fisherman, whose first language was Aramaic, could have produced it? Though many reply, "No," the better answer is, "Why not?" Recent studies reveal that Galilee was bilingual. Almost certainly Peter would have spoken Greek, as the language of trade.

And we must not discount the effect of 25 years of mission in a Greek-speaking environment—nor the influence of Silas, who helped Peter to write the letter (5:12).

If by Peter, then this first letter was written from Rome (5:13—"Babylon" is a code for Rome) at a time when there were Jewish Christians throughout the Roman provinces listed in 1:1. These two factors give the letter a date perhaps in the late 60s. Early Church tradition puts Peter in Rome for the last part of his ministry. The letter is addressed, like James, to "the Dispersion," an expression for Jews scattered around the world, who are Peter's particular mission responsibility (Galatians 2:7).

Peter's readers

Persecution is clearly looming (1:6-7; 3:13-17; 4:12-19; 5:9-10). Peter knows that his readers feel

The theater, Hierapolis, seat of Papias.

isolated and vulnerable. They are "aliens and exiles" (2:11, compare 1:1). Peter skillfully modulates this sense of social alienation into the idea of election: they feel different because they are different (2:9).

Jews in Asia Minor were well integrated into local culture, and many of them participated happily in local festivals, as Peter reminds them (4:3). But now they have stepped back, and incurred suspicion and hostility as a result—especially by refusing to participate in the imperial cult by which people expressed their gratitude and loyalty to the emperor. Slaves and women were particularly vulnerable, for it was culturally unacceptable for them to adopt a religion different from the male head of the household. So Peter gives them special encouragement in the so-called "Household Code" (2:13–3:7).

Overall, Peter seeks to inspire his readers with a vision of what God has done for them in Christ, and to encourage them to "do good" in every situation, however difficult (2:12-14, 20; 3:6, 11; 4:19).

John

The letters of John do not identify their author by name, but the ancient manuscripts all include a heading which names "John." As in Hebrews, the opening greeting is missing from the first letter, but

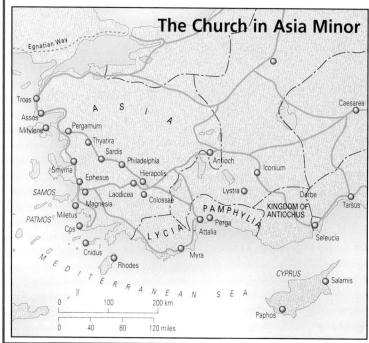

The Church in Asia Minor

Egnatian Way

Troas
Assos
Mitylene
A S I A
Pergamum
Thyatira
Sardis
Philadelphia
Smyrna
Ephesus
Hierapolis
Laodicea
Magnesia
Colossae
Antioch
Iconium
Lystra
Derbe
Tarsus
Caesarea
SAMOS
PATMOS
Miletus
Cos
L Y C I A
P A M P H Y L I A
Perga
Attalia
KINGDOM OF ANTIOCHUS
Seleucia
Cnidus
Rhodes
Myra
CYPRUS
Salamis
Paphos
M E D I T E R R A N E A N   S E A

0   100   200 km
0   40   80   120 miles

The remains of the Temple of Artemis (Diana) in Ephesus, with (*inset*) statue of Artemis.

etters 2 and 3 are written by someone calling himself "the Presbyter" (2 John 1; 3 John 1).

Uncertainty arises at this point, for Papias (bishop of Hierapolis *circa* A.D. 135) distinguished two 'Johns" among the first-generation Christians known to him: the Apostle and "the Presbyter." So, even if the author was indeed "John," we do not know which! But the parallels in theme and style with the Fourth Gospel support the traditional view that John the Apostle wrote these letters in Ephesus toward the end of his long life. Letters 2 and 3 are addressed to particular churches over which "the Presbyter" has authority (3 John 9), but letter 1 may be generally addressed to all the churches in the greater Ephesus area, or more widely still.

The two great themes of John's letters are love and truth (see 2 John 1-3). Both are firmly fixed to Jesus Christ, which gives them a particular spin. The great issue in the first letter, for instance, is the departure from the Church of a group whom the author calls "Antichrist." They have denied love because they have broken off from their fellow believers, and thus must be "in the darkness," separated from God Who is the light. Fellowship with God is only possible for those who are "in the light," which means living in fellowship with one another while "the blood of Jesus His Son purifies us from all sin" (1:3, 7; 2:9-10, 18-19).

But this means that a denial of love is also a denial of the truth (that Jesus Christ, by His death for us, binds us into fellowship with Himself and with each other). And in the case of this group, their denial of the truth is signaled by their explicit denial "that Jesus is the Christ" (2:22; 4:2-3). This probably refers to the idea, associated with Cerinthus in the late first century, that "Jesus" and "the Christ" were separate beings: the former an ordinary man, the latter a spiritual being who descended upon "Jesus" at His Baptism, but departed again before the Crucifixion.

> It is better to suffer for doing what is right, if such is the Will of God, than for doing what is wrong. For Christ also suffered for our sins once for all, the righteous for the unrighteous.
> 1 Peter 3:17-18

James, Jude, and 2 Peter

James and Jude belong together in that these two letters are both ascribed to "brothers" (which indicates close relations, perhaps cousins) of Jesus (see Mark 6:3). Jude and 2 Peter belong together in that there is considerable overlap of material between them. Clearly one has used the other, although it is not clear which!

Who are the authors?
The traditional authorship of all three has been disputed, although the arguments for pseudonymity are strong only in the case of 2 Peter. This little letter is quite unlike 1 Peter and had some difficulty being accepted as genuine in the early Church. It may reflect a later period in its attack on the false teachers (chapter 2). In addition, it seems at pains to prove its genuineness, including references to the life of Peter (1:16-18) and to "our beloved brother Paul" (3:15).

The stylistic differences from 1 Peter are not, however, incompatible with common authorship, especially if Peter and Jude were using a common source or working together in composing the attack on the false teachers. The questions intertwine, for if Jude is genuine then 2 Peter is likely to be genuine, for it is highly unlikely that a later writer would use it so fully in producing a pseudonymous letter ascribed to Peter. And Jude *is* likely to be genuine, for a pseudonymous writer would be unlikely to choose so obscure a figure as Jude, or to write something so short, or to characterize Jude as a "servant" rather than the "brother" of Jesus (see Jude 1). So the early Church was probably right to set doubts aside and accept both as genuine.

Jude
We have no idea where Jude ministered, though we know from 1 Corinthians 9:5 that "the 'brothers' of the Lord" had itinerant ministries. Possibly, while James led the church in Jerusalem, and Peter traveled west, Jude went east to the Jewish communities in Parthia, Media, Elam, or Mesopotamia (cf. Acts 2:9). If these letters are genuine, then we must imagine Peter and Jude becoming deeply concerned—possibly at the same time—about the influence of a "libertine" movement.

The false and the true
Paul tackles this libertine teaching in 1 Corinthians 6:12-20. It rested on a dualistic conception of human persons, and taught that because the soul (the real, inner self) has been saved completely by Christ, and can no longer be sullied by the "flesh," we can do what we like with our bodies. Gluttony and debauchery are back on the menu! Jude and 2 Peter

Ruins of the ancient black basalt synagogue at Chorazin near the Sea of Galilee.

The death of James

Ananus, who . . . had been appointed to the high priesthood, was rash in his temper and unusually daring. He followed the school of the Sadducees, who are indeed more heartless than any of the other Jews . . . when they sit in judgment. Possessed of such a character, Ananus thought that he had a favorable opportunity because Festus was dead and Albinus was still on the way [that is, there was a vacuum of power between two Roman governors]. And so he convened the judges of the Sanhedrin and brought before them a man named James, the brother of Jesus Who was called the Christ, and certain others. He accused them of having transgressed the law and delivered them up to be stoned. Those of the inhabitants of the city who were considered the most fair-minded and who were in strict observance of the law were offended at this. . . .

Josephus *Antiquities* 20:199-201

A coin dating from the Jewish revolt, with the only known depiction of Herod's Temple, Jerusalem. James continued to lead the Jerusalem church in worship there until his death.

xpress sustained horror at this eaching: for Jude, it amounts to a denial of "our only Master and Lord, Jesus Christ." (4; compare 2 Peter 2:1). They both insist that this is not the authentic Christian way (Jude 17-18; 2 Peter 3:2-3). Peter gives a moving defense of true Christian morality, which he builds upon intimate relationship with God (2 Peter 1:3-9), and upon the transformation of the world by Christ at His coming (2 Peter 3:10-18). He argues that both of these provide a moral imperative for transformation now.

James

James is likewise passionately concerned with practical issues of Christian life. His letter is vivid, direct, and uncompromising, presenting essentials of Christian discipleship with an emphasis on prayer, how to cope with suffering and the testing of faith, care for the poor and the dangers of wealth, and the control of the tongue.

A strong argument in favor of the traditional ascription to James, the "brother" of Jesus, is the way in which the letter coheres with what Josephus, the Jewish historian, writes about James. He describes James's martyrdom in A.D. 62 at the hands of the High Priest Ananus, who hated him and seized an opportunity to have him executed in the "gap" between two Roman governors. Just before this time, in A.D. 59, there was rioting in Jerusalem caused by the oppressive behavior of some Sadducean families, like that of Ananus, toward the poorer priests. Tithes were seized and some priests actually starved to death. In light of James 4:1–5:6—and 2:14-17—it is not hard to imagine what James said about this, and how he thus made enemies in high places.

An attack on Paul?

James 2:14-26 has caused much discussion, with its apparent attack on Paul's doctrine of justification by faith. Whereas Paul taught that Abraham was "justified" by faith and not by "works," James says the opposite: "Was not Abraham our father justified by works when he offered his son Isaac on the altar?" (2:21).

Some maintain that James is issuing a warning against Paul's teaching, just as it was "some people [who] came from James" who argued that the Gentile Christians in Antioch should obey the Old Testament law (Galatians 2:12). But we must take seriously Galatians 2:6-9, where Paul reports unanimity between himself and the Jerusalem leadership, including James (cf. Acts 21:17-26).

James could be attacking a distortion of Paul's teaching. Paul taught that one could only be justified (at peace with God) by faith. He did not teach that one's responsibility ended there. He spoke of having to "work out" one's salvation. One had to express one's faith through one's good deeds (which did not buy God's love but were rather a response to it).

Revelation:
A Book for the Millennium

The New Testament ends with one of its most remarkable books: "The Revelation [or Apocalypse] of Jesus Christ" (1:1), a colorful, evocative, awe-inspiring "removal of the veil" between heaven and earth (this is what "apocalypse" means), making events on earth transparent so that their real, hidden dynamic becomes clear. And, as the title suggests, "Jesus Christ" turns out to be that dynamic. Behind everything that happens lies the story of Jesus Christ: His Incarnation, suffering, martyrdom, rising and exaltation to heaven, gift of the Spirit, and ultimate coming as Judge and Savior.

Type of writing
In form, Revelation is a letter from "John" (1:1, 4, 9; 22:8) to the seven churches of Asia, who each receives a brief letter from Christ Himself (chapters 2–3), but to whom, in fact, the whole Apocalypse is addressed (1:11; cf. 22:16). In genre, it is a prophecy (1:3; 22:7,10,18), because it involves "witness to the Word of God" (1:2) by John: it is revelation from God.

Temple of Trajan, the acropolis, Pergamum.

Remains of the Temple of Artemis, Sardis

We must imagine it being read aloud, at one hearing, in each of the churches (1:3), and this must affect the way we interpret it.

The writer
This "John" is probably not the Apostle, because the Greek style is completely different from that of the Gospel, with which the Apocalypse has little in common. But he is clearly known to all the churches —he needs no more introduction than just his name—so perhaps he is Papias's mysterious "John the Presbyter."

The province of Asia
The Roman province of Asia enjoyed a period of great prosper-

The ancient agora, Smyrna (Izmir).

ity in the first century (see 3:17). Revelation 18 pictures the vast network of Mediterranean trade depending on huge numbers of merchant ships, by which imperial Rome sustained her power and wealth. But this prosperity came with a price tag: it involves trade in "human lives" as well as the luxuries of the East (18:13).

The two beasts
John does not just mean the slave trade. No one can buy or sell, he tells us, without "the name of the beast" stamped upon them (13:16-17). Careful reading of chapter 13 suggests that the two beasts are, respectively, Rome, which enslaves the earth and makes blasphemous claims, persecuting the Church, and the imperial cult, by which the ideology of Roman power was promulgated and

Some of the remaining stone arches of the stadium, ancient Laodicea, Asia Minor.

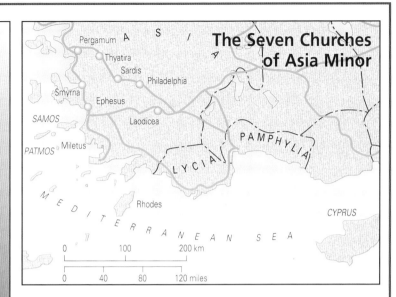

The Seven Churches of Asia Minor

nforced. The cult of the goddess "Roma," or of the current emperor, was particularly strong in Asia centered on Pergamum, "where Satan is enthroned," 2:13). It was impossible to engage in the export or import trade without involvement in the imperial cult.

The message to first-century Christians

So the prosperity of the seven cities is built on the selling of their souls to Rome through their commitment to the imperial cult, and, in the name of Christ, John wants to call the churches to "depart from her, my people, so that you do not take part in her sins" (18:4). The message of the book thus has a strong relevance for the first readers, and this should probably check any propensity to find esoteric meanings far removed from their circumstances. As with all letters, the first challenge in interpretation is "What did it mean?" before further questions about later or contemporary significance are asked.

The message to all Christians

At the same time, however, the very fact that the Roman Empire is portrayed as a symbol—the beast from the sea—encourages us to ask where else this symbol might fit. Where else do we see totalitarian power, which opposes the Church of Christ and seeks to control people's minds by an all-embracing ideology? John would encourage us to see the power of

The Library of Celsus, ancient Ephesus.

the dragon behind all such situations (12:9–13:2).

The prophecy is presented as the narrative of a single visionary experience, not a series of separate visions like Daniel. The book thus has a powerful structural coherence and dramatic movement. The seven letters in chapters 2–3 are the first of several series of "sevens," which are carefully structured and follow on from each other. The message of the seven letters—that Christ knows His Church, holds her in His hand, and directs her destiny—turns out to be true for the whole world. So in the face of apparent chaos, persecution, and weakness, the Church can look behind the veil, hear and join the worship of heaven, and see the glorious destiny toward which the world is being steered (11:15; 21:1–22:5).

The New Testament could hardly end in a more fitting way. It begins with a Baby called Jesus born in an obscure corner of the Roman Empire. It ends with the nations walking by His light, and all the kings of the earth surrendering their glory to His (Revelation 21:23-24). The movement from one to the other is the story—and vision—of the New Testament.

Index

Nihil Obstat: Rev. Donald E. Blumenfeld, Ph
Imprimatur: ✠ Most Rev. John J. Mye
    J.C.D., D.D., Archbishop of Newark

Copyright © Angus Hudson Ltd/Tim Dowl
& Peter Wyart trading as Three's Compa
2000

Worldwide co-edition produced by Li
Hudson plc, Wilkinson House, Jordan H
Road, Oxford, OX2 8DR, England
Tel: + 44 (0) 1865 302750
Fax: + 44 (0) 1865 302757
Email: coed@lionhudson.com.
www.lionhudson.com

First published in 2000 as *The Student Gui*
Introduction to the New Testament.

Published in the United States in 2008 by
Catholic Book Publishing Corp.
77 West End Road
Totowa, NJ 07512
ISBN: 978-0-89942-652-5
T-652
www.catholicbookpublishing.com

Printed in Singapore

Picture acknowledgments
Photographs
Tim Dowley: pp. 7, 11, 12, 14, 16, 24, 25, 2
29, 30, 32
Jamie Simson: pp. 5, 13, 19
Peter Wyart: pp. 3, 4, 5, 6, 17, 18, 20, 26, 31, 3

Illustrations
Alan Parry: pp. 3, 22
Richard Scott: pp. 10, 21, 23
Paul Wyart: p. 8

For Further Reading

New Testament

R. Brown, *The Churches the Apostles Left Behind* (Paulist, 1984)

E. Lohse, *The New Testament Environment* (Abingdon, 1976)

P. Perkins, *Reading the New Testament* (Paulist, 1988)

The Gospels

R.A. Burridge, *What Are the Gospels? A Comparison with Graeco-Roman Biography* (Cambridge University Press, 1992)

Richard Bauckham, *The Gospels for All Christians. Rethinking the Gospel Audiences* (T & T Clark, 1998)

Matthew

G.N. Stanton, *A Gospel for a New People. Studies in Matthew* (T & T Clark, 1992)

R.T. France, *Matthew, Evangelist and Teacher* (Paternoster, 1989)

Luke

I.H. Marshall, *Luke, Historian and Theologian* (Paternoster, 1970)

J.A. Fitzmyer, *Luke the Theologian. Aspects of his Teaching* (Geoffrey Chapman, 1989)

C.M. Tuckett, *Luke* (Sheffield Academic Press, 1996)

John

S.S. Smalley, *John, Evangelist and Interpreter* (Paternoster, 1997)

R. Brown, *The Community of the Beloved Disciple* (Paulist, 1979)

S. Motyer, *Your Father the Devil? A New Approach to John and "the Jews"* (Paternoster, 1997)

Paul's Early Letters

N.T. Wright, *What Saint Paul Really Said* (Lion, 1997)

C.K. Barrett, *Freedom and Obligation. A Study of the Epistle to the Galatians* (SPCK, 1985)

J.R.W. Stott, *The Message of Thessalonians* (IVP, 1991)

1 and 2 Corinthians

J.D.G. Dunn, *1 Corinthians* (New Testament Guide: Sheffield Academic Press, 1995)

L.J. Kreitzer, *2 Corinthians* (New Testament Guide: Sheffield Academic Press, 1996)

Romans

R. Morgan, *Romans* (New Testament Guide: Sheffield Academic Press, 1995)

A.J.M. Wedderburn, *The Reasons for Romans* (T. & T. Clark, 1988)

Paul's Later Letters

K.P. Donfried & I.H. Marshall, *The Theology of the Shorter Pauline Letters* (Cambridge University Press, 1993): includes Philippians and Philemon

Hebrews

Barnabas Lindars, *The Theology of the Letter to the Hebrews* (Cambridge University Press, 1991)

A. Vanhoye, *Our Priest Is Chris The Doctrine of the Epistle t the Hebrews* (PIB, 1977)

Peter and John

Judith Lieu, *The Theology of th Johannine Epistles* (Cam bridge University Press, 1991)

J. Ramsey Michaels, *1 Peter* (Wor Biblical Themes; Wor Publishing, 1989)

James, Jude and 2 Peter

A. Chester & R.P. Martin, *Th Theology of the Letters o James, Peter, and Jud* (Cambridge University Press 1994)

Revelation

S. Doyle, *Apocalypse: A Catholi Perspective on the Book o Revelation* (St. Anthony Mes senger, 2005)

Richard Bauckham, *The Theology of the Book of Revelatio* (Cambridge University Press 1993)